I0698680

CASH ON DEMAND

How To Raise $1000 In 30 Days, Without Borrowing Or Selling Off Your Properties

KINGSLEY OKORO

The Kings Organization

Copyright © 2023 Kingsley Okoro

All rights reserved

No part of this book may be reproduced, or stored in a retrieval system,
or transmitted in any form or by any means, electronic, mechanical,
photocopying, recording, or otherwise, without express written permission
of the publisher.

ISBN: 9798873479931

Contact us: +234 703 210 2369
Email Address: kingsorg84@gmail.com

CONTENTS

Title Page

Copyright

INTRODUCTION: 2

STEP ONE: 11

STEP TWO: 24

STEP THREE: 30

STEP FOUR: 35

STEP FIVE: 41

LAST LAP: 51

58

CONCLUSION:

BONUS ONE: 60

BONUS TWO: 68

MEET THE AUTHOR 73

CASH ON DEMAND

How To Raise $1000 In 30 Days, Without Borrowing Or Selling Off Your Properties

BY KINGSLEY OKORO

INTRODUCTION:
YOU WILL NEVER GO BROKE AGAIN
AFTER READING THIS BOOK

Imagine you received a call and it's from a family member. There's a need that has to be met in the family and you are required to provide $1000 to solve this need.

You have just 30 days to raise this money, and the worst part is, your salary won't be due in another 30 days. Even if salary was to come now, it would be nowhere half that amount.

Or maybe you just got a notification on your phone and it's a text message from your landlord reminding you that rent would be due for renewal in 30 days. Your rent is $1000, but for certain unplanned reasons, you haven't kept any money for this.

Or maybe you have a business plan you've written and you need $1000 to launch the business. You are excited about your idea. You are hopeful of the great things you will accomplish through this business. Yet, no one has agreed to invest in your dream or to support you.

Imagine you find yourself in any of the above situations, or any situation at all that requires you raising $1000 in the next 30 days; the question is, what would you do? Do you have any means of raising $1000 to take care of the situation between now and the next 30 days?

The truth is most people don't. For many people, the only source of income they have is their job or the small trade they've managed to establish for themselves. There is no source of income that can generate money on demand for them.

If you are someone like this, that's okay. You don't have to feel bad about it because you are not alone. Many people work really hard to earn a living, yet they are almost always broke or struggling financially. And the truth is; it is not always their fault.

Taking a look at the economy of Nigeria and most countries right now, you'll understand that your chances of enjoying a financially free life is almost impossible if your only means of making money is by trading your time for money.

Having other means of earning money will provide you more options in life. You will be able to afford better lifestyle for your family and you will be confident enough to switch careers or pursue other goals whenever you desire to.

Most especially, you will be in a better position to support your family with money; even if the demand is a little urgent.

This is what this book is written to help you with. My goal is to show you how to create more options and to enjoy financial independence. Independence means you are able to do what you want to do, whenever you want to do it. It means you are able to quit your job if you feel you don't enjoy working there anymore, without being afraid that your family would go hungry.

And most of all; independence means that you can come up with new ideas and you'd have both the time and financial means of working on your idea...or at least, you know how to create the money to fund your ideas.

Learning how to create money on demand is something anyone can do. It does not require certain level of academic qualification, ethnicity, or background. Anyone can become a living printing machine who can create money whenever they need it.

If you read to the end of this book, and you apply what I will show you, I guarantee you too will become a living printing machine, creating money from nothing, and enjoying full financial independence.

The Biggest Mistake People Make

One mistake people make when thinking of making more money or having another income source is that people suddenly declare themselves "investors" overnight; or they simply hand over their hard earned money to someone they believe is a good investor and pray their money does not get burnt.

In other words, most people simply start looking for ways to multiply their money; so they take their life savings and put into some so called investment opportunity that promises huge returns.

You probably have been a victim of this before now. It's okay. You're not alone. Millions of people have lost their life-savings and many have even committed suicide when they suddenly lost the money they thought would make them more money.

Robert Kiyosaki would always say, "Investing is not risky; investing without being an investor is risky."

In other words, being an investor takes skill, experience, and a great deal of money. You can't simply take up money you spent months or years saving and invest into something you have no control over.

Before trying to be an investor—before trying to multiply money—you must first learn how to create money. You need to be sure that even if you lost an investment, your family won't go hungry because of it.

You need to know that investing could go right or wrong, but having ability to create money will keep you on your feet, even when everyone else is down.

Multiplying money is too risky for you if you do not have ability to create money.

Knowing how to create money is the foundation of financial intelligence. Knowing how to multiply money and keep it growing (through investing) is the secondary level.

People lose their money because they tend to skip to the secondary level, when they don't have the foundation in place yet.

Without a solid financial foundation in place, many people would find it difficult, or impossible, to bounce back when they lose their money through wrong investment. This is why many commit suicide the moment their investment crash.

This book is NOT about investing or multiplying money. It is about showing you how to create money. It is about increasing your ability to make money whenever you want it. It is about establishing you at the foundational level of financial intelligence.

How Much Money Do You Want To Make Monthly?

Regardless of how much you earn today, you can make more money. In fact, you can make ten times more money than you are making today, every month.

You can increase your income by any level you desire. All you need to do is learn how to create more income streams. The person making ten times your income today isn't super human. He simply has something you don't have yet: CAPACITY.

The difference between what you earn right now and what you dream of earning is capacity. To make that level of income, you just have to increase your capacity to make more money. Find out what people who are earning higher than you know and do that thing. Do not settle for your current income; increase your capacity to make more money.

How To Build Capacity

You build capacity through Personal development.

No matter how little you earn today, if you don't learn to invest part of that into developing your skills and increasing your income capacity, you will remain at that income level for a very long time.

Investment in yourself is the greatest investment you could ever make. Learning skills that can help you create more income will pay off in the long run than any other thing you choose to do with your money.

I'll say that again: Learning skills that can help you CREATE money whenever you need it, is a much more valuable investment you could ever make, than any hot crypto deal, or real estate deal, or forex deal flying around the internet promising to make you rich overnight.

Here's a reality most people don't pay attention to: Everything you have right now can be taken away from you. Your job can be taken away. You could lose your car, your house, your spouse, etc.

Recently in Nigeria, we have witnessed a high level of property demolition by the government in various states. These are high mansions developed with people's years of

hard work, sweat and tears being demolished to the ground and turned to dust right before their very eyes, and there's nothing they can do about it.

A major shift in the economy, or a change of policy by the government, can wipe out your savings and investments. We see this happen almost every day and it will continue to happen to many more people. But do you know what no one can take away from you, for as long as you live?

Your SKILLS! The skills you have learned will remain with you for life. And if you are wise enough to learn what I call "MONEY PRINTING SKILLS", then your survival will never be threatened.

So, instead of looking for the next big deal in crypto, or stock, or even real estate to invest your money into; I recommend you first invest in YOURSELF. Increase your capacity to make more money and you will be happy you did.

How To Create Money From Nothing

The first time I created money out of nothing was back in 2020. The Covid-19 pandemic had hit and everywhere was on lockdown. Businesses were grounded and money wasn't flowing.

People were afraid and food was scarce. I had a network marketing business I was doing at the time and because of the lockdown, business was slowed down.

While I was still able to promote my products and opportunity leveraging social media, most of my team members weren't. And this affected both their income and mine.

I started thinking of how to help them. The more I thought of it, I began to notice that many other network marketers I knew had the same difficulty. This included both people in my company who were not my team members, and other networkers from different companies.

Because they were no longer able to go out into the streets to prospect like they used to, or to go from one physical seminar to the other, or to invite prospects to their physical seminars, their businesses seemed to be grounded.

This became a problem I decided to help solve. I decided I was going to teach these people how to leverage social media, especially Facebook, to keep their business growing.

All I did was to write a simple eBook to teach people how I do my business online without needing to hit the streets or meet people physically or even attend physical meetings.

This appealed to many network marketers and they bought my book. I made more money selling that book than I was making from my network marketing business at the time.

It was a great feeling because this money was created out of nothing. I only shared knowledge I already had. It also cost me nothing to create this income stream. I created the eBook using my smartphone and sold many copies of it.

People were just paying and downloading my book, even while I slept. I sold to people from Nigeria and other neighboring countries and I made a lot of money.

Ever since then, I have enjoyed the art of creating money out of nothing. I first heard that line from the famous American rapper, Lil Wayne. He said, "I made something out of nothing; so thanks to nothing".

I fell in love with that ideology of making money out of nothing. I wanted so much to experience it at all cost, and when that opportunity showed up, I took it.

Whenever you find yourself in a problem that requires money to solve, that problem is simply asking you: WHAT CAN YOU DO?

In other words, the problem is there to test your ability. It is there to shine a spotlight on your strength or weakness. Problems simply come to test our capacity to create solution.

How This Book Will Help You

There is money everywhere. No matter where you are right now, you can find money everywhere around you, if you know how to identify it.

The reason people struggle financially, even when money is everywhere, is because people have not been taught how to identify money lying right under their nose.

This book is a step by step guide to help you see money where you are and also grab as much of it as you can. This is a "project" to help you create money out of nothing like I did. I want to walk you through the process of raising up to $1000 in the next 30 days.

This is an action-oriented book. I am not here to share theories. It is straight to the point.

What you will find here are 5 workable steps that will take you from where you are right now, to where you will have at least $1000 in your account—money you created following my 5 steps.

So, if you are ready to create money out of nothing, then let's dive in.

STEP ONE:
DECIDE WHAT TO GIVE IN EXCHANGE FOR THE MONEY

You want to raise $1000 in 30 days? That's okay. You also want to raise this money without begging anybody for money, or asking for a loan, or even selling off your properties.

But here's one thing you must know: The money you're looking for will come from people.

Even though you are not going to beg anybody for money, you still have to find a way to make people raise you the $1000 you are looking for.

The money you need is not hanging on a magic tree somewhere. It is not hiding in one website. It's in the hands of people. And the only way to make people give you their money is to give them something in exchange.

No, I'm not talking about auctioning off your jewelries or cloths, or your gadgets, like most people do when they need money. I am talking about selling a product that people will gladly buy from you because it solves their pressing need.

You want to provide solution to people's problem because that is the only way to make them willingly give you their money. So right now, what you need to do is package this solution you have into a product that people can pay for.

A restaurant owner is solving a problem of hunger and he packages this solution into a product called "food".

A musician is providing entertainment to help people stay happy and he packages this solution into a product called "Music".

A teacher is helping people defeat ignorance and increase capacity and efficiency, so he is delivering this solution via a product called "knowledge".

A doctor helps people fight diseases and stay healthy. What he is rendering is called "medical services".

Do you get the point now?

So the questions you should ask yourself are: "What problem do I want to solve?" "How do I deliver the solution so people can gladly pay me?"

Choose a Niche

If you want to make a lot of money, you have to choose a problem that appeal to a large number of people.

And if you intend to stay relevant for a very long time, choose a niche that will always stay relevant regardless of how the economy goes.

The reason I didn't start out selling cloths is not because I didn't like cloths or the clothing business is not a good business. It is rather because I understand that most people only think of buying new cloths when they feel they have some extra money to spend, or when they have a function that needs a certain kind of outfit.

A person may feel the need to change his wardrobe, yet won't buy a single cloth for a whole year if he has more important and urgent needs to take care of.

The reason I went into the healthcare business and the education business is because I knew that people will always spend money on these two areas whenever they have need for it.

When you fall sick, you can't ignore it to do something else just because you don't have much money. You can't say, "I would've loved to get treated, but I'm saving this money to change my car". Nobody does that!

You spend even your last money to get medical treatment, because you know that money in the bank, or a new car in your garage, won't mean much to you if you can't get up from your sick bed.

When you want to improve sales in your business, you will gladly buy a course or pay for a training or buy a book that teaches you how to achieve your sales goals. This is because you understand that without sales, you will soon be out of business.

When you feel the need to make more money—and most people have this need—you will gladly pay for knowledge that can help you increase your income and live the life of your dream.

So choose carefully which problem you want to solve and set up a product or service that solves that problem well. That's what people are going to be paying you for.

Your choice of product should appeal to a large audience and must address a growing need. That is how to make money for the long term.

Narrow Down Your Niche

Your niche must be specific, if it must attract the attention of people who will pay for it. You have to think of a specific problem you want to solve and focus on it rather than dwelling on a wide niche and confusing people.

For example, "Healthcare" is a wide niche. But if you say your niche is "weight-loss", or "Sexual health", or "Fertility"; that's a good niche because you have narrowed it down.

"Money Making" is also a niche, but it is too wide. But when you say, "Sales", or "Cryptocurrency", or "Real estate", you are narrowing down to a specific audience that you want to help.

Narrowing down your niche will help you single out the specific people you are trying to help and pass your message to them. It will help the right people to easily connect with you and pay attention to what you are offering. It also portrays you as an expert in your field.

What Kind Of Product Should You Sell?

There are many kinds of products you can sell to make money online, but for the purpose of this project, we'll be using an intellectual product, or digital product.

This means a product that teaches people to do something, or provides knowledge or answers to specific needs. A product you can easily create and deliver online without having to meet people face to face, or without always having to package a physical product for delivery each time someone orders for it.

Examples include an eBook, a video tutorial, an online course, or even a Live online class.

If you want to raise $1000 in 30 days, this is the fastest, easiest, and cheapest way to achieve this. I would know this because I've done it several times.

In 2020, during the Covid-19 lockdown, I was able to use a piece of eBook I wrote to raise over $1000 from the comfort of home.

I did this without spending a dime of my own money and I have repeated it over again, including using Live classes and online courses. So I know exactly what I am saying when I say this is how you create money out of nothing.

What this means is that you are going to create an educational product where you will teach people how to solve a particular problem. And this must be a problem that people are looking for how to solve.

If your niche is Weight-loss, this means you could create an eBook, or a tutorial video, or even a course, where you teach people how to lose weight within a particular time-frame, without going through the usual stressful procedures they hate to go through.

Or if your niche is Sales, then you could create an eBook, or a single training video, or a course, where you teach people how to skyrocket their sales and increase their cash flow, using a simple procedure that guarantees better result.

Or if your niche is Sexual Health, you could write an eBook teaching men some simple exercise they could practice, or diet they could eat, or herbs they could take; that will improve their erection or sexual performance.

Believe me, millions of men are desperately looking for solution to this problem and they'd gladly buy whatever product that promises to help them out of this frustrating and shameful condition.

Or create a course that'll teach women how to reach orgasm faster. Because, trust me, a lot of women, including women who have been married for years and even have children, have never experienced what orgasm feels like.

So if you think you have the solution to this, you can package an educational product, or even organize an online class where you'll expose this secret to them.

These are just examples of products that can bring in cash flow immediately, if you do it well. But feel free to create a product in your specific niche, around the specific need you have identified.

And make sure your product delivers on the promise. Because the last thing you want is people paying for your product and ending up not getting what they paid for.

Why Digital Products Are Your Best Option For Creating Money From Nothing

1. It's easy to start – Once you have knowledge you can teach, you don't even need to have money to invest in it.

I created my first eBook with my smartphone and sold it from my smartphone. If you have a laptop, it makes things a lot easier for you.

2. No recurring costs – Once you write your book or create your course, you don't have to recreate them over again whenever someone wants to buy.

Once created, a course or eBook can be bought by thousands of people and it never expires unless the knowledge you teach becomes obsolete.

3. The market is large – Knowledge is something people will always pay for. And since you're using the internet, there's no limit to how many people you can reach with your product.

You could create a product that is purchased by people from different cities, states, or countries.

4. You set your own price and profit – The economy does not decide how much you sell your product; the value of your product determines that. You have the power to make your product as expensive or as cheap as you want.

I have seen online courses sold for $10 and I have seen online courses sold for $500. People have organized 3 days live class and charged $500 for it.

And after the class, they kept reselling the replay from the class. The profit potential is enormous. Just have value to offer.

5. You never run out of stock – The same eBook or Course that sold only 50 copies can still sell 10,000 copies if you figure out a way to market it to more people. The limitation of running out of stock, which is common with physical products, is never seen in digital products.

6. You help more people – Creating digital products is not just about making money for yourself; it is also a means of helping more people. Let's say you're an expert in creating graphic designs for small businesses and you've been doing this and getting paid for your service.

You know there's a limit to how many people you can really help. But by creating a course or holding a class to teach small business owners how to create simple designs with their smartphones, you'll be able to help many more people, while making more money.

7. A lifestyle of freedom – Being a digital creator gives you opportunity to work from anywhere. You could decide you don't want to stay in your city and just pack up and move to somewhere else the next day, without worrying about your business being affected.

Since you can create digital products from anywhere you are, you have a lifestyle of freedom that most people only dream of.

8. Easy to create, sell and deliver – If you've ever tried creating physical products, you'd know it's not easy. From production costs, to government registrations, to risk of damages, to storage space, etc., you have a lot to worry about.

But with digital products, you don't worry about any of these. And if you're smart enough to know how to automate your selling and delivery system, you can literally make money while you sleep.

9. You can start making money quick – There's nothing stopping you from setting a goal to make $1000 in the next 30 days and achieving that goal. Creating a physical product and bringing it to market can take a long time.

And you also have to worry about the risk of not making enough sales to cover the cost of production. That is not so with digital products. You can start making money and profits on the same day.

From the time I decided to write my first eBook to the day I launched and started selling it was literally less than 2 weeks.

10. Multiple Income Streams – If you already have a job or business, you can decide to work in your spare time creating a digital product to generate additional income.

And if you've created an eBook that is making you money, there's nothing stopping you from creating a video course also to make more money.

In fact, once you keep your eyes and ears open to see the problems people have that you could help teach them how to solve, you can create and own as many digital products as you want and make thousands, or even millions, each month.

Decide How To Deliver Your Solution

If you have decided what problem you want to help people out of, the next question is, "In what format should your product come?"

You have to decide if an eBook, or a single video tutorial, or an online course, will work best for what you hope to teach. You must also consider what works best for you, what style of communication you feel you can do better.

There are people who communicate better via writing and there are people who communicate better via speaking. If you understand what works best for you, then you already know what format your product will have, whether it is an eBook or a video.

And if you choose a video, then decide if you feel more comfortable showing your face while teaching your audience or you feel more comfortable speaking behind slides.

Whichever style you choose, what matters is that your delivery must be good enough that your audience can get value.

Your eBook does not have to be voluminous. 10 to 15 pages is already large enough. I have bought some eBooks that had only 8 pages and the value was great. I have also bought an eBook that had over 100 pages, but it didn't meet up to expectation.

So that's where your focus must be—value. It is value that people paid for, not the volume of the book or the length of the video training.

Don't get into the illusion that if your course contains as much as 30 videos, then people will be happy to buy. Or if your book has hundreds of pages, then you've done a great job.

Most people don't read voluminous books and most people don't have the patience to finish a 30-video course, unless the value is super great and the teaching is captivating.

Focus on delivering the best value. Focus on solving the problem you have promised to solve with your product. Focus on making sure that when someone buys your product, they'd end up happy that they got real value from it. That's the goal!

Don't Complicate The Process

I have seen a lot of people hold themselves back from creating digital products and making money from their knowledge simply because they are waiting to have all the gadgets and software they've seen other people use. Don't waste your time on all that. Use what you have.

When I wrote my first eBook, I did not own a laptop. I didn't even have a great smartphone, but at least, I owned a smartphone and I did everything on that phone.

From writing the book, to designing the cover, to publishing the eBook and selling it, everything was done on my smartphone. It was an old Infinix x510 I was using at the time.

Of course, using that phone wasn't very easy and a laptop would've made the process much easier, but my point is I didn't let a lack of laptop or a more sophisticated smartphone hold me back.

If I was waiting to have all the sophisticated gadgets, I probably would still be waiting till now. Today, I use a laptop and a much better smartphone, but that is possible because I was willing to start with what I had at the time.

The only way to make progress is to start with what you have and then upgrade as the money starts coming. Waiting won't change anything for you; only ACTION will.

As long as your smartphone can operate a Word document, that is all you need to write a book. As long as you can use Canva to design your book cover, or create slides for a video course or tutorial video, you are good to go.

Summarizing Step One

1. Think about a problem you want to solve. Think hard about this. If this is in an area you already have a skill or expertise; that is much better.

For example, if you are already a chef, you could decide to teach people how to make certain kinds of meal, or you could teach people some healthy meals they could eat to avoid some predominant health challenges like diabetes or hypertension or obesity. You could also teach people some uncommon recipe that will take their kitchen game to the next level.

So think hard about what you want to offer and make sure it's a niche that has a large audience. Also, make sure your product is addressing a pressing need. Emphasis on "pressing need". Because if the need is not pressing, most people won't take it seriously.

A lot of people can put off buying a book on how to dress elegantly. While it is important to know how to dress elegantly, many people have more pressing needs they're worried about than stepping up their dressing.

A pressing need is a need that people are desperate to solve. Conduct a little research to make sure what you have chosen has a hungry market.

2. Determine what format your product will come in. We discussed four options: an eBook, a single tutorial video, an online course, or a Live class.

Any of the formats will work. Personally, I love eBooks because I love to write and eBooks are easy to create. It doesn't cost me anything to create an eBook and I can do everything myself.

Videos are also great. In fact, recording a tutorial video is a lot easier than writing a book, plus I don't even always have to show my face while teaching. I could easily hide behind beautifully designed slides I created on Canva.

Creating an online course may be a lot more tasking because you have to record more than one videos and you have to organize them in modules. But I also love courses because people would naturally pay more for a course than for an eBook.

The idea is to choose what works best for you and your target market and create your product.

3. Don't hold yourself back. Don't wait to have all the fancy gadgets or software before you start.

People don't really care how sophisticate your intellectual product is. All they care about is whether you deliver on your promise or not.

If you have something the world is longing for, you shouldn't deny them of it merely because you don't have the means to make it classy. Just do it!

STEP TWO: GET SERIOUS ON SOCIAL MEDIA

This is a very important step you must take immediately after deciding to create a digital product or to make money online. Your social media handles must communicate to people that you are an expert in your niche.

Most people don't know that their social media profile speaks a lot about who they are. People will always check you out online before deciding to buy from you or work with you.

So this step is about doing some important work to ensure that the next time someone visits your Facebook profile, or your Instagram profile, they'd feel like they want to know you more.

Here Are Some Things You Can Do Now:

1. Clean up the dirt! For most people, their social media handle contains a lot of rubbish, both from them and from other people who tagged them. You must start from sanitizing your profile and timeline.

If you have been posting things that could jeopardize your chance of being seen as an authority online, you have to start deleting them now. You must delete as much as you can find. Go back as far as you can.

Don't just delete yours; delete every posts you were tagged that is on your Timeline and endeavor to change the setting to make sure future posts you are tagged to doesn't just appear on your Timeline without your consent. Your Timeline should not be a dumping group for everyone who has something to post.

If the post does not concern you directly, or if it doesn't have anything to do with your niche—if it is not something that adds to your credibility in the minds of your audience—then delete it and free your Timeline of all the junk.

They say to not judge a book by its cover, but when it comes to social media, people will definitely judge you by what they see. If they think you are an unserious person, they'll never buy what you are selling.

2. Upgrade your profile! If your Profile photo does not show quality, change it. You can go get a professional photo from a studio to put on your Profile. It's that serious. A professional photo taken from chest up is suitable for your Profile. It speaks a lot about how intentional you are.

If you have accounts on different social media platforms, use the same professional photo as your Profile photo on all the platforms, it will make it easier for people to identify you.

Don't use a photo you took with your spouse or kids. Don't use a full picture of you. Profile photo should be from chest up and it must be you alone in the picture.

Not just your Profile photo, the Cover photo too should be professional. But for the Cover, you can design something with Canva that talks briefly about you and what services you render.

Write a short, captivating, straight-to-the-point Bio that tells people how you can help them, or highlights what you do. Be professional.

"About" section should also contain vital information that tells people about you, where you work or what company you own. Completely revamp your social media Profile to present you as a professional. Visit the Profile of those influencers and experts you admire online to get inspiration from how they did theirs.

3. Give Value! The reason step two comes immediately after you have decided on the niche you want to focus on is because it is important that before you create a product and ask people to buy, they must have known you as an expert or an authority in that niche.

People will only buy your product if they have already seen you as an authority in the area you're talking about. It's called the KLT Factor (Know, Like and Trust).

Having people who Know you as an authority on a particular niche, and they Like the way you talk about it, and they already Trust that you know this so well and can deliver on this niche any day, will help increase your chances of having them buy your product when it's finally released.

This is why you must begin to do this now…before you even begin to create your product.

What this simply means is you must start posting valuable content on social media daily, and 80 percent of this content must be centered on your niche.

So, if your niche is Weight-loss, for example, you need to make out time daily to write content on social media that talk about weight-loss. You must begin teaching people what you know and what you are learning about weight-loss and about living healthy.

Again, follow other top experts online and see how they post daily. You can post more than 3 times a day, but make sure majority of your posts is on your chosen niche. This is how to make yourself the go-to person on this subject.

You must engrave your name and face in the minds of people so much that whenever they think about your niche, your name is the first thing that comes to their minds.

4. Build up your capacity! See, you can become as good as you want to be in your chosen niche. You can become so good that when you speak about it, people follow you.

And the easiest way to achieve this is to be intentional about learning and growing.

Just because you know some things about weight-loss doesn't mean you can't learn more. You are now an expert on the subject, so do all you can to live up to that title.

Read more about your niche. Buy books around your niche and read them. Go online and do research. Go on YouTube and learn from other experts in that niche. Buy courses and learn from other experts.

Also, remember to teach as you learn. Teaching is another form of learning too. When you teach, you learn twice.

So share lessons on social media about what you are learning. Hold free classes from time to time to give value for free. Build your capacity and carry your audience along. Let people know how passionate you are about this niche and how much you love to help people in this area.

Building up your personality online is a very important foundational step you should take, even before you have a product to sell. This will make it easier for people to buy from you, even before you start investing in marketing.

Post online daily. Post multiple times daily. Post on Facebook, on Instagram, on WhatsApp status, and even in Facebook Groups you belong, especially Groups that has the kind of people you need, people who might be interested in your niche.

5. Engage in other people's content! Don't be a selfish person who wants others to engage with your content but you won't read other people's posts or engage in them.

When you engage in people's posts, you are making them feel good and you are also making yourself popular with them. Whenever they see your content, they'll naturally engage too.

Also, the algorithm works in your favor when you take time to engage with people's content.

The algorithm automatically assumes you know these people, so it will make sure you always see their posts at the top of your Newsfeed, and they'll also see your posts at the top of their Newsfeed.

So take like one to two hours every day to read people's post. Don't just like them, leave comments too. Intelligent comments will always stand you out.

You can gain loyal followers just because of a brilliant comment you left under someone's post.

I have gotten followers on Facebook just because I left some comments in some posts I saw in a group I belong. Most people follow me and even DM to let me know they followed me because they liked my comment on that post.

Social media is a place to connect with people. It is a place to build relationships. Don't joke with opportunities to build quality relationships online.

STEP THREE:
START CREATING YOUR PRODUCT

You have chosen your niche and you've decided what problem you want to solve with your digital intellectual product. You have even put your social media handles and Profiles in order. You are now building authority around your niche.

You've also decided the format you'd like to deliver your solution in—an eBook, a course, a single training video, or a recurring online class.

Now is time to start creating your digital product. It's time to put together that solution in a product that people will pay you to help you raise $1000 in 30 days.

The first thing you should do here is to sit down and write out the benefits you want to offer your audience through this product. Write out everything they stand to gain from reading your book or watching your training.

Remember that what people will pay for is the benefits of your product. If you're writing a book or creating a course, what the reader or student hopes to get is knowledge that will help him solve his pressing need. So list out those benefits.

Writing out the benefits will help you know how to arrange your lessons to cover everything you have promised your audience. You need to ensure your product delivers the promise.

After writing out the benefits in details, the next thing is to list out the lessons and arrange them serially.

If it's an eBook, list out the chapters and sub-chapters. If it's a course, list out the modules and lessons in each module. If it's a single training video or an online class, list out the lessons you want to teach accordingly.

Your goal is to take the people step by step, from one level to the other, until you have delivered everything you promised. This process will help make your work easier and more organized.

Start Creating The Product

After this, start creating the product. Start writing the book. Start recording the training.

You can write a simple eBook or record a full video course in 3 days. Remember, you are not trying to create something voluminous or lengthy that will bore people; you are creating a straight-to-the-point, concise resource loaded with value.

For an eBook, write on a Word document. This can be Microsoft Word, Google Doc, or any word document you have. You can download it online if you don't have it already.

For video training, I like to design a slide on Canva and then record the training using a screen recording software I have on my laptop called "Camtasia". You can find any screen recording app on your app store, if you are recording from your phone, or simply record it via Zoom and save the video.

Alternatively, if you don't mind showing your face while teaching, that's another good way to record your teaching, especially if using a slide is not compulsory for what you are teaching.

You can simply set your phone camera to yourself and record while teaching. You can even keep a white board and teach using a marker.

My point is; the style of recording is not as important as the value you are giving your audience. What people are paying you for is not the style of recording. People are paying for value; so give them the value.

The most important thing when recording a training video is your sound. People will forgive you for having a lousy picture quality, but they won't forgive you for having a lousy audio quality.

Invest in sound, if you have to. You can buy a lapel microphone —the one you clip to your shirt—and connect it to your laptop or phone to improve the audio quality of your training video.

Next is to edit the book, or video. Carefully proofread your book to correct every error. Give to someone who is good in English to help you with the editing. Pay a professional editor if you have to. Ensure your book is devoid of grammatical or typographical errors.

Design your book cover using Canva. That's the easiest place to do it. Canva already has lots of eBook cover templates you can use, if you don't know much about designing.

You can also design your eBook layout using Canva to make it more professional. But if that would be too much work for you and you can't afford to pay someone to do it for you, don't worry yourself. You can still publish your eBook straight from the Word document.

The first eBook I wrote was published direct from MS Word on my phone. The only thing I designed on Canva was the book cover, which I downloaded and inserted to the book on MS Word before converting it to PDF via Google Drive. It's that simple.

If you recorded a training video or video course and you think there is no much error, then there may be no need for editing. But if there are parts of the video you don't think is good enough to be there or you think is not necessary, a simple trim, split and join is enough editing. Nothing sophisticated.

You don't have to be a pro video editor…I am not! I simply use Inshot app or CapCut app to edit on my phone. I also use Camtasia to edit and export if I recorded slides using my laptop. Don't complicate it, keep it simple.

The main difference between a single tutorial video and a video course is that a single video tutorial, as the name implies, is just one video. It can be 30 minutes long, or 1 hour long, or even 3 hours long. But it's just one video that delivers a complete training.

A course, on the other hand, contains multiple videos. A course is a more comprehensive training divided into sections usually called "Modules". Each module can also be divided into lessons.

If you think your training needs to be divided into small multiple videos that takes students from one level to another, then a course is best for this. But if your lesson can be delivered in a single video, then go for a single tutorial video.

But remember, people naturally would pay more for a video course than for a single training video. I don't know why, but this is how it is.

As soon as your product is ready, you're almost ready to start cashing in on it. You are already on your way to raising $1000 using this single product. So let's move to the next step.

STEP FOUR:
SET UP A DELIVERY SYSTEM

How would you deliver the product when people pay for it? There are many ways this can be done, but I prefer to use a system that makes it super simple.

If it's an eBook, it is very simple. You can easily send it to them via WhatsApp for straight download. Or give them a link to go download the book wherever you uploaded it.

This could be your Google Drive or any other platform available to you.

Personally, I like to use Selar. This is a platform that does everything, from collecting money from the buyer to delivering the eBook for them to download directly.

You can even set your eBook for people to read it right there online rather than downloading it. This is only necessary if you want to prevent people from sharing your eBook with their friends without your consent.

But it's usually best to let people download the eBook and read it whenever they want, and Selar helps out with that.

You can create an account with Selar.co and you will have your own online store on the platform immediately. Proceed to create a product, insert the price, write a description that will tell people what they are buying and then publish it.

When someone comes to your store, they can go through your description, learn about what you are selling and then click on "Buy Now". They'll be prompted to enter their name, email address and phone number and then, they'll make payment right there.

As soon as Selar collects the money, the buyer will automatically be redirected to where they can get the eBook. If you have uploaded the book to the platform for easy download, they can download it right there.

But if you have entered your WhatsApp link instead, they will be redirected to your WhatsApp DM where you will give them the book yourself.

This strategy is good if you are looking to have the contacts of those who bought your product for future purposes. You can also enter a WhatsApp Group link where they will be redirected to get the product.

If you created an online course or tutorial video, you have an option of uploading it to your YouTube channel and setting it to "unlisted", so that the only way a person can watch it is if they have the video link.

I have used YouTube to host a full course with over 15 videos. You just have to create a "Playlist" and upload all the videos to that Playlist. The Playlist link becomes the link you give to anyone who buys your course. Once they click on the link, they'll have access to the entire videos in the course the way you arranged it.

The disadvantage of hosting a video course on YouTube is that a person can buy your course or training video and decide to give the link to other people. Some people might even be reselling your course without your consent since they have the link to the course.

Another disadvantage is that YouTube can decide to ban your account if they think your videos are violating any of their rules. This is something you don't have control over.

Alternatively, you can upload your videos on Selar, the same way you do an eBook, and have Selar deliver the product to those who pay for it. This way, you're not afraid that anyone will steal your product or resell it without your consent. Your videos are safe and protected on Selar.

The only problem is that this is not available if you are using the free version of Selar. If you are selling an eBook, you can sell as many books as you want using the free version. Selar will only take their little commission whenever someone buys, and you can even set it up in a way your customers pay this commission so your money isn't touched.

But with the premium version, you can host your video course or tutorial video and have them access it right there on the platform when they pay. It makes the whole process easy and keeps your product protected from unscrupulous people.

There are many other options available, including hosting your product on your own website. But I am showing you the easiest systems I've used and still using. As I write this, the premium version of Selar begins from N8000($20) monthly. And if you decide to pay for a whole year at once, you get a handsome discount.

On Selar, you can even decide to set up an affiliate program where other people can market your product and earn commission on each sale they make. This is a good way to increase sales effortlessly.

Selar is also good because you'll be creating more digital products in the future. You can have as many products as you want selling on your Selar store.

So, what if you are organizing an online class? Well, you also have options.

The easiest place to use is a WhatsApp Group. In a WhatsApp Group, you can teach using either text or voice clips. I prefer voice notes because it's more convenient, both for me and my students.

With WhatsApp Group, I can also pre-record my teachings into short clips using my phone recorder and deliver them during the class as though it was being delivered live.

All you have to do is create a WhatsApp Group and add people there when they pay for your class. You can set up the payment on Selar and include the Group link so whenever someone pays, they are automatically redirected to join the Group.

Alternatively, you can add people directly to the Group yourself after they have paid. This is also good for those who would be paying via bank transfer instead of card payment on Selar.

Keep the Group closed and only open it when the class starts to avoid disturbance from people.

Another way to deliver a class is via zoom. You can create a zoom meeting and share the invite link with those who paid for your class. This can also work together with a WhatsApp Group.

Simply add everyone who paid to your WhatsApp Group and then drop the meeting link in the Group when the time comes so they can join the meeting. A Live training on zoom can be recorded and downloaded later for future use.

The third option is to create a Private Facebook Group and use it for your class. I love this strategy too because the training can stay there for others to join the group later to watch. So, with this, you can keep selling the class to new people and simply adding them to the Facebook Group to watch the training replay.

A Live training held inside a Private Facebook group can also become a course you continue to sell for as long as you want. All you have to do is make it a 3 days Live training or a 5 days Live training.

After the training, more people who didn't join it live can continue to pay for the training to be added so they can watch the replay. This is another way to make money repeatedly from a training you held once.

When it comes to collecting payment for your product, always give at least, two payment options. First I'll set up a card payment via Selar. Then I'll also add a bank account for transfers, in case anybody has a reason they can't do a card payment online. Don't give people a reason to not buy your product.

If you add a bank detail for transfer, remember to include a WhatsApp number they can send payment proof to, so they can get access to what they paid for.

So, your product is ready and the delivery system is set to deliver to those who buy. Now let's talk about the last step to follow to raise $1000 in the next 30 days.

I believe this next step is the most important step of all, because without it, your product will not generate money for you. So let's take care of it.

STEP FIVE:
MARKETING THE PRODUCT

Having the best products or services won't mean much for you if you cannot get people to buy.

It is one thing to know that your products solve a major problem. It is another thing to know where to find those people who need your products. It is yet another thing to make these people believe in your products and to buy them.

This is why developing your ability to sell is no longer an option; especially if you want to stop being broke.

Knowing how to sell is a must. Knowing how to sell online is even better. And if you ever want to create a consistent pool of cash flow, you must know how to develop a simple marketing system that keeps customers coming.

There's something I always say to my students. You can go broke with any profession if the economy becomes very bad. But a person with good skill in sales can pick up anything and turn it into cash flow. All he has to do is look for what need people are facing at the time and sell them the solution.

The reason I am emphasizing on this is because I know that many people turn the other way whenever they hear the word, "selling". They act like it's not their thing.

Most people are even terrified of selling. They'd do whatever they can to avoid getting involved. This is why people prefer to give money to strangers promising quick investment returns.

They know it is risky, but they would rather take that risk than getting involved in a business that requires them selling something. And every business does require selling—selling is what brings in money.

So, instead of running away from selling, I suggest you LEARN. No one was born a sales person. People learn to sell. And as far as learning goes, what makes it effective is practice. This means you must be willing to step into action.

In this step, I will show you how to follow a simple marketing system that will turn your product into consistent cash flow.

At the end of the day, the goal is not just to help you sell this product you have created right now; the goal is to turn you into a person who can pick up any product tomorrow and turn it into money. That's the greatest skill you could ever have in life.

1. Put a price on your product! The first step is to decide how much you are to sell the product you just created. Put a price tag on it. There's no rule of thumb here. Your product can sell at any price, as long as the value of your product is more than the customer is paying for it.

I have seen people sell a simple eBook for $10 and I have seen people sell a whole video course for $2. It all depends on your income goals at the moment.

But before you slam a price on your product, it is important to know what your income goal is. Knowing your goal will guide you on how much you need to put on the product and how many people you need to sell it to, to achieve your goal.

For this project, our goal is to raise $1000 in 30 days. So the question is, how many people do you have to sell to, at what price, to reach the goal of $1000 in the next 30 days? So let's do a simple math to give you a guide.

Let's say you're selling an eBook or a course and you put the price as low as $2. Does selling your product as cheap as $2 guarantee you will reach this goal faster? Let's see.

Most people will argue that keeping your product very cheap will guarantee fast sale, since it become easy for people to buy, no matter their income level. They may be right, but what is the cost to you, if your product is as cheap as $2? How fast can that price help you reach your goal of raising $1000?

At $2 each, how many people do you need to buy your product, in order to raise $1000? The answer is 500 people. Sounds pretty easy, right?

But how many people do you need to expose your offer to, in order to get the 500 people who will end up buying?

If we are to follow statistics, then we'd be working with a 10 percent success rate. At 10 percent rate, the number would be 5000 people. You have to show your offer to at least 5000 people, in order to have 500 people buying from you.

These numbers are not absolute. They can change for different people. But according to experts, only about 10 percent of the people who see your offer will buy immediately.

So, the question is, how do you get 5000 eyeballs to see your offer? How much will it cost you in advertising fee to reach that number of audience?

Let's see another example. Let's say your product is tagged at $10, how many people do you need to sell to before you hit $1000?

The answer is 100 people only and you would only need 1000 people to see your advert to reach the 100 buyers who would give you the $1000 you're looking for, following the success rate of 10 percent.

Do you see the huge difference? This is why running your numbers is important before deciding the price of your product. You can't just price your product the way you see others doing, or because you think selling it too cheap will make people buy. You need to work with your income goal.

Let's take a final example on this. Let's say you are selling an online course for $20, how would that impact your goal?

At $20, you only need 50 customers to reach your income goal of $1000 and to reach 50 buyers; you would have to show your marketing to 500 people only.

You might think an online course is too expensive at $20, but that's because you're just starting. I have paid $100 for an online course and I have seen people selling their courses at $499 and people buy them. So it all depends on the value you're giving and also the level of influence you've built over time.

Am I saying that selling your product as cheap as $2 is bad? No! I'm only saying to run your numbers and decide what you hope to achieve and what it will cost you to achieve it.

If you feel your product is worth $2, then go ahead and sell it. If you feel like making it cheap so you can use it to generate enough leads you will sell to in the future, that's also a good strategy.

2. Announce your product on social media! You've been giving free value to your audience and you have built a good reputation for yourself. Now is time to sell something that your audience will buy.

If people have been enjoying your content and they've confirmed it through their comments and likes, there's a high chance they'll trust you enough to buy your product. So you have to announce it to them.

Go on Facebook and write a good post about the product you just created. Talk about all the benefits they'll gain if they buy your products and tell them how to buy the products.

Design a beautiful graphic image on Canva displaying your product and attach it to your post. Let them see what you are talking about. You can get someone to help you with this if you don't know how to.

Take this same post and share it on other platforms you belong: Instagram, Twitter, WhatsApp Status, etc.

There are people who follow you on these platforms that believe in you because they've been consuming your valuable content for a while. Some of them may not even have commented on your posts, but the moment you announce a paid product, they'll buy.

If you had created a WhatsApp broadcast list where you

share valuable content with people, you can also share this announcement to let them know you have released a product they should buy.

3. Run paid ads! Announcing your product on social media is one way to show people what you have and kick off sales of your new product, but it is not the only way to guarantee sales.

You could make a few sales this way, but unless you are as influential online as John Obidi, or Emeka Nobis, or Mute Efe, or Eno Sam, or Ijeoma Dicta; you may not generate enough sales to reach your goal of $1000 in 30 days by just posting on your social media handles.

You need a more guaranteed marketing system that will generate sales on demand and that is by running a paid advert that generates targeted leads to your product.

There are three components that make a marketing system effective: Traffic, Offer, Close.

Traffic is simply talking about the number of people who comes to see what you are selling. With a paid ad, you can have thousands of people coming to check out your product, which increases your chances of recording enough sales to reach your income goal of $1000 in 30 days.

If you know how to target the audience well, you will be attracting only people who have an interest in what you are offering, as opposed to posting on your Timeline without knowing if they are interested in your offer or not.

For example, if you are marketing a product that appeals to only women within a certain age bracket, living in certain locations; you can achieve that using paid Facebook and Instagram ads. This will help make your marketing more specific and guaranteed to generate sales.

If you don't know how to set up an ad campaign, you can learn how to. Simply go to YouTube and find some free training videos that will teach you how to run ads. You can also pay an expert to run the ads for you so you don't waste your ad money.

Generating enough traffic will ensure you have enough eyeballs seeing your product, which is critical to achieving your income goal faster.

The next component is your offer. How you write your ad copy is important, if it must convince people to buy. Focus more on the benefits people will get from your product.

Put a lot of effort on the headline. Your headline will determine if people will even read the rest of your ad copy or not. Make sure your headline is captivating enough to make someone stop scrolling to check out what your ad is talking about.

Writing a headline that says, "How To Lose Weight Fast" is too lame and won't raise any eyebrows. But when you say something like, "5 Simple Steps To Lose 10lbs In 30 Days, Without Dieting Or Going To The Gym Everyday—Guaranteed!"

That is a more compelling headline. It is powerful enough to make someone stop scrolling to read the rest of your copy. It's disruptive and interruptive.

First you have indicated that there are 5 steps and they're simple. Then you indicated a number of pounds they will lose in just 30 days. And you have also indicated that they won't have to diet rigorously or hit the gym.

That is what we call disruptive marketing. Whatever you are selling, think hard before writing your headline. An expert said that when you write your headline, you've spent more than 50 percent of your ad money.

Your ad copy is also very important. I suggest you study other peoples copy to see how they wrote theirs. Make sure your copy talks more on what they stand to gain.

If you're using a landing page, then write your copy to sell the click. Selling the click means that the goal of your ad is to make people click on it and land on your landing page where they will see the whole story and your offer.

But if you're not using a landing page and you are selling direct from your ad, then be as detailed as possible in explaining what they stand to gain when they buy.

Your offer must be compelling too. You must make them believe the amount they are paying is nothing compared to what they are getting. This is why most marketers add bonuses to their offer.

When trying to sell to people, do not focus on talking about the product. Talk more about the problem the person is having and how this product will help solve that problem. Make the prospect see why not buying this product would be the biggest mistake he would be making today.

Adding a bonus, like an extra free eBook, or a free membership to your VIP mentorship group, or a free video training, will help increase the value of what you are selling.

When people feel like what you are offering is so valuable that the amount you're asking for it is a bargain, they'll most likely buy.

Another thing you can add to your offer is a kind of urgency. You can tell them the discount price or the extra bonuses will only be available for a limited time or to a limited number of people. This will make them buy immediately because they don't want to miss out. That is a smart way to close your sale.

One final strategy I'll talk about, which you can use to sell your product is to organize a free WhatsApp class and run your ad to market the free class, instead of running the ad to sell your product directly.

This is beneficial because most people don't know you yet. You want to build credibility first before asking for their money. So putting together a free class will help you build credibility.

More people will click to join a free class than to buy a product from someone they know nothing about. Remember that people easily buy from someone they KNOW, LIKE and TRUST, so give them the opportunity to get to know you, like you and trust you and a great way to achieve this is by taking them off the crowd, bringing them together in a room and giving them a taste of the value you have.

If you've ever walked by a suya stand, you'll notice that one thing most suya sellers normally do is offer you a free taste of their suya. They do this because they are most convince that the moment you get a taste and like it, you'll most possibly buy from them. This is the same strategy you'll be using when you organize and market a free class before selling your product.

If you deliver great value in your free class, they'll easily pull out their wallets to buy your paid course or eBook. It works all the time. It is easier for someone to buy your product after you've given them a taste of value you can offer; as opposed to asking them to buy your product the first time they're seeing your ad on social media.

A free WhatsApp class or Zoom class is a great way to sell. It is called "selling with classes". You can repeat the process as many times as you want, until you hit your income goal.

LAST LAP:
BRINGING IT ALL TOGETHER

So, let's bring everything together to simple actionable steps you can begin to follow now. Let's get busy raising the $1000 in 30 days.

Step One: Choose the problem you want to solve. Take a look at the skills you have now, the expertise you have and the knowledge you have. Do you think people have a pressing need that you can teach them how to solve with that knowledge, or skill, or expertise?

I know a business lawyer who started teaching small business owners how to implement good legal systems to their businesses to protect them from legal errors that could cost them lots of money. She teaches these through her various eBooks, online courses and Live classes.

I also know some people who are good in writing. They create products to teach people how to write good books and how to sell their books. It's a major problem they're solving and making money from.

I know people who sell educational products teaching people how to cook certain meals, or how to market their products online, or how to run ads, or how to edit videos, or how to attract the right man for marriage.

There's a hunger for knowledge in virtually every niche. Find yours and plug yourself in there. Do more research online to find out what pressing need people are having in that niche. Find out what questions people are asking about that niche. Get into the conversations already going on.

A simple keyword on Google search bar will give you a list of enquiries people are making online about that topic.

Choose the format of your product. Decide if you're writing an eBook or creating an online course or a single video training or holding a class. Choose what works best for you and your audience.

Step Two: Get serious online. Social media is a great tool for business; don't take it for granted. Clean up the dirt on your profile. Make sure your profile presents you as an expert in your niche.

Start giving value in your chosen niche. Start sharing free helpful information that teaches people what they need to know in that niche. Be intentional about your activities online. Show up every day. And remember to engage in other people's content.

Invest time and money in yourself. Build capacity. Buy courses and books. Upgrade your knowledge and skill. Read blog posts online around your niche. Watch YouTube videos around your niche. Intentionally get better at what you do, so you can serve people better.

Step Three: Start creating your product. Write out the lessons you want to teach and organize them in chapters, or modules, or sections. Make it easy for you to follow accordingly when you begin to write or record.

If you've been giving real value on Facebook, some of your posts can become content for your book or course.

Design your slides on Canva if you are creating a video with slides. When it's time to record, you can record direct from Canva on your laptop, using a screen recorder like Camtasia, or Zoom.

If you are using a smartphone, install a screen recording app that can record your presentation. Don't wait. Just do it.

Write your book on MS Word, whether on your phone or laptop. Edit it carefully, or pay a professional editor to prevent errors that could undermine you.

Design your cover on Canva. You can design the book layout on Canva if you know how to, or just arrange it properly on your Word document.

Edit your videos with Inshot or CapCut or Camtasia. Just create that product.

Step Four: Set up a delivery system. Create an account on selar.co/ and upload your eBook there. You may need to upgrade to the pro version to be able to upload your training video or course on Selar. Otherwise, just host your videos on YouTube and set it to "Unlisted" so only those with the video link can access it or simply upload it to Google Drive and share the link with buyers.

Create a Playlist on YouTube and upload your videos in the Playlist if you are creating a course. Arrange the videos accordingly so people can easily watch one after the other.

You can also create a Private Facebook Group and upload your videos there. Anyone who pays for your training or course will be added to the group and only the admin can add people to the group.

This is also a good way to protect your videos from people who might want to share or resell them without your consent. For online Live class, you have options to choose from. A WhatsApp Group where you teach using text or audio clips. A Zoom meeting where you invite those who paid for your class to watch you Live. A Facebook Group where you add people and teach them using a Livestream.

The meeting on Zoom can be recorded, downloaded and uploaded somewhere else, like a Facebook Group, to sell to more people. Your Livestream in a Facebook Group will stay there and you can continue adding more people to go watch the replay as they pay you.

With many options available today, there's no reason you shouldn't start selling your digital product and making your money.

Step Five: Set up a marketing system and start selling your product. Start by putting a price on your product. Do the math to know what price is best for your product.

A product of $2 may be easy for people to buy, including people who don't have much money. But you will need to sell to 500 people to reach your goal of $1000.

A product of $20 may look expensive for most people, but you only need to sell to 50 people to hit your income goal of $1000.

So, do your checks and balances and decide how much you should ask for. Make sure the value they get exceeds the amount they're paying, so you don't end up with angry customers who will never buy anything from you in the future.

Next is to announce your new product on Facebook, Instagram and WhatsApp Status. You can also send to your email list or your broadcast lists on WhatsApp if you have them.

If you have been giving free value to these people over time, there's no reason some of them won't start buying your product immediately.

You can even start talking about your product weeks before it is ready. Let them expect it beforehand. You can offer a special discount to those who want to pre-order the product beforehand. This is how to start selling your product even before it is ready.

As long as they believe in you and your product promises to give great value and solve a pressing need, your contacts will be happy to grab the opportunity of getting it at the early bird discount rate.

Don't just settle for free marketing. Invest in paid ads so you can reach even more people who might be interested in your product.

With paid ads, you can target the type of people you want to see your ad: the age range, the location they reside, and other things that increase your chance of getting the right customers for your product.

Pay attention to your headlines. Don't just write a headline casually. Study other headlines. Go online and research how to write a compelling headline.

Your ad copy is also very important. Don't spend much time talking about the product; rather, talk more about the benefits they stand to get if they buy and what they stand to lose if they don't buy.

Talk about the problem they are having and emphasize on their pains. Then promise them the future they are hoping for and assure them that your product will give them that future.

Increase the value of your product by adding some bonuses to your offer. You can make the bonus only available for a limited time or to a limited number of early action takers. This will create a sense of urgency as nobody wants to miss out on a chance to get something extra for free.

Finally, to help build up confidence in your audience and take away doubt, you can run your ads to promote something free, and then sell your product later to them. I like to sell with free online Live classes.

Teach something of great value in the free class, and then introduce your product to them at the end. If you have given value for free, they'll believe your paid product will definitely give them much more value.

As you make sales, continue to reinvest in your ads until you generate enough money to reach your income goal.

For example, if it cost you a total of $100 in ads and other expenses, then your revenue goal should be $1,100. this will ensure that your net income from this project remains $1000.

So go ahead and follow the steps and start counting your money.

CONCLUSION: JUST DO IT

Raising $1000 in 30 days is as easy as following the steps I have taught you in this book.

These are steps I follow to raise money, which is why I have no need to look for a job or beg people for financial help. Knowing how to raise money will help you stay financially afloat, even when many others are drowning in debt and lack.

I have just handed you the power to create money out of nothing; the only thing standing between you and $1000 in the next 30 days is your willingness to get up and start taking action applying what you've learned in this book.

If you don't take action, nothing I wrote here will make any difference for you. But if you start now, following the steps as I laid them out for you, then you will certainly celebrate your $1000 in the next 30 days.

And after reaching that goal, feel free to continue selling that product and making even more money. Also, feel free to create more products as you identify more needs that you can help people solve.
I started this book by announcing that money is everywhere, but people complain of being broke because they have not been taught how to identify money and grab it.

I believe that now, you are no longer like most people. I believe you can now see money lying around you and you already know how to get as much of it as you want.

So right now, I wish you the best as you begin your journey into the world of knowledge money. I hope to hear your testimony soon.

Sincerely,
Kingsley Okoro

BONUS ONE:
FIVE TIPS FOR SELLING OUT
YOUR DIGITAL PRODUCT

As a bonus, I want to give you five powerful tips that can help you sell out your digital products easily. If you follow them, I believe you will record massive sales and make a lot of money.

TIP #1: PACKAGE YOUR PRODUCT WELL!

I have mentioned earlier that people actually do judge a book by its cover. The way you present your product will determine if it will attract people's interest in the first place.

When it comes to relationship between a man and a woman, people think that physical beauty is not as important as character.

But I believe that for a man to be attracted to a woman in the first place, physical beauty must have played a role.

Because if a man's attention is not attracted first, how would he get to know anything about the woman's character?

Likewise when it comes to selling your digital product, people's attention has to be caught first, before they will even get a chance to check out what you are selling to decide if it's for them or not.

So pay attention to your packaging and presentation. Start from your title.

The title you give your book or course must call out to your target audience. It must be disruptive enough to stop someone from scrolling past to check out what you are talking about.

People have very short attention span, and if your title can't grabs someone's attention the first time they see it, they may never get to check out the product or to read your sales message to decide if they want this or not.

That is why you can't just name your product carelessly. It must either arouse curiosity or intrigue, or announce a benefit, or highlight a fear. Make sure that just by seeing the title; they will get an idea of what they could gain from buying that product.

And not just your product title; also incorporate this strategy when writing the headline for your marketing.

Whether you are writing the ad copy or the sales latter for your landing page, endeavor to make it intriguing and captivating enough to keep them glued to read the rest of your marketing message.

Another thing to pay attention to is the design, especially for an eBook. Make sure the design is beautiful and attractive. Hire a professional designer to do this for you, if you are not very good at it.

Designing also include your marketing image or graphic. Use a good mockup image to present your product to make it exude quality.

And if you're creating a marketing video for your product, make sure you're not camera shy, ensure your English is sound and understandable, do not use too much grammar, and endeavor to cut out parts of the video that are not necessary before using it.

If you present your product and your marketing well, a person who never had a budget to buy anything can reach out to their wallet and buy your product. Your presentation must be that powerful.

TIP #2: CREATE EXPECTATIONS BEFOREHAND!

Start talking about your product while still creating it. Share excerpts from your book or training on social media and let them know it's coming from your upcoming product.

You can even find a way to carry your audience along and make them feel like they are part of the process. Strategies like posting two different cover designs and asking them to choose which one they like best for your book is a good strategy.

You can also write three to four different titles and have them vote for the one they feel is more captivating. You can create a poll and have your audience vote which they love most.

As you write your book or create your course or prepare for your class, continue to talk about it on social media. Register it on the minds of your audience to create expectation.

You can create a waitlist and ask those who are interested in getting your product first to join the waitlist. You can give something in return for joining the list; for example, a price slash or a special class for those who join the waitlist.

Creating a waitlist is very simple. I use a WhatsApp group for my waitlist. Continue to remind members of your waitlist of what to expect as the launch date is drawing near.

TIP #3: STACK UP THE VALUE!

There are many people who will not buy unless they feel like they're cheating you. And by that, I mean that they will respond more when there's much more to gain than to lose.

The internet is already saturated and every day, these people are bombarded by marketing ads from other creators promising to change their lives. They have many options to choose from, so give them more reasons to choose you.

Add other rated products to your main product as bonuses. Make sure these other products are equally as valuable, or even more valuable, than the main product. Make them feel like this is a steal—like they'd be losing out on so much if they don't buy this product.

When talking about your bonuses, attach the value of each bonus for them. Let them see how much you are willing to give out to them for free, just for buying your product.

Remember that these are all digital products; so you won't be losing anything by giving them additional products for free. Rather, this will increase number of people who will buy your product.

If you are selling a course, you can write a 5 to 8 page eBook and add as a bonus. You can also record a 30 minutes training video where you teach another valuable lesson that will help them get the result they want better.

My rule of thumb is to ensure your bonus products are all centered on the problem your main product is solving. It has to be something that helps to make the original product even more valuable.

For example, if your main product is teaching how to satisfy your woman as a man; you can create something else that exposes 10 kinds of meals that is weakening their sexual performance and what they should eat instead.

This one alone can make them buy your product, because they would want to know what these common meals they may have been eating are and what better meals they should be eating to boost their sexual health and performance. Apply this strategy in any niche you're in; it works all the time.

TIP #4: CREATE URGENCY!

A lot of people are indecisive. They know they want this, but they can't seem to make up their minds to buy it now.

They may be contemplating getting it later; but you know what they say about the "I'll do it later" attitude? It's that "later" often becomes "never".

So help them make that decision now. And the best way to do it is to create a sense of urgency. Give them a reason to take action now or lose something.

You can announce a special discount for early action takers and put an expiry date to it. Let them know that once this date or time elapses, the price goes back up to its original.

You can also announce that your additional bonuses are only available for a limited time period, or to a limited number of people. Let them know that once the deadline is reached or that number of people buys, you are taking off the bonuses.

Humans respond faster when there is a tiny window for getting something. Nobody wants to miss out, so give them a reason to take action now.

TIP #5: BUILD A LIST!

Now, this is important, both for selling out this product and for selling out future products without spending much on marketing.

List building is the smartest thing you can do for yourself as a business owner. I once heard Brian Tracy say that even if you take away everything he owns today—his houses, cars, businesses—he will get them all back within a short period because of the quality list he has built over the years.

Your list is a collection of people who know you and have been following your message overtime. They believe in you and your ability to help them; that's why they are there.

Any product you market to these people will experience good sales turnover, depending on how large your list is. This is why it is important to start growing your list even before you have a product to sell.

The best platform for building a list is Email Marketing. But if you don't have what it takes to grow an email list now, you can start with alternative options like WhatsApp Group, WhatsApp Broadcast, Facebook Group, Telegram Group, Telegram Channel, etc.

You are in a business called "Attention Arbitrage". This means the number of attention you can command will determine the level of money you can make online.

Social media is a crowded place. Your ability to move your target audience from the crowded social media and bring them together in your list, where you continue to nurture them with value daily, will increase your chance of selling out any digital product you announce later.

The fastest way to get your target audience to join your list, whether it's your email list or your WhatsApp Group, is by giving out something for free as bait. In digital marketing, this is called "lead magnet".

You can organize a free class to be held inside your Facebook Group or WhatsApp Group. Or you could give out a free eBook or video training.

The goal is to get people who are interested in getting this free value to join your list and become members of your community. Hence, you must ensure the free stuff is within the scope of your niche.

Conclusion

Those are my five tips that can help you sell out whatever digital product you create. The goal is to ensure that you don't struggle to hit you income goal after going through the process of creating that wonderful product.

Do your best to apply these tips, in addition to everything I talked about in this book, and I guarantee you will be smiling to the bank soon.

Cheers!

BONUS TWO:
HOW TO RAISE MONEY BY
ASKING FOR HELP

I know the title of this bonus chapter contradicts the essence of this book, which is to create money without begging, borrowing or auctioning off your belongings. However, there's a reason I decided to share this little trick I have used to help some people in the past.

Let's say you've recorded an online course, and you want to host the course on Selar, but you would need to upgrade to a Pro version to be able to do this. Let's say this is money you don't have, what do you do?

As I write this, the starting price for Selar Pro is $20 a month. Not much money, but let's say you don't have any money now, would you let this hold you back?

Most people will allow this hold them back, but I don't want you to be like most people, which is why I want to share a little trick with you.

Let's also talk about the fact that you would need money to run a Facebook ad to market your course. Let's say your plan is to pay $5 a day for 30 days to run your ads simultaneously on Facebook and Instagram.

$5 a day for 30 days is $150. Add that to the $20 for Selar Pro and you have expenses of $170 waiting for you. How would you raise this money?

Well, if you remember, I have already given you one option in step five, which is to promote your product to your audience and have them pre-order it beforehand. If that goes well, you can raise money to host your course on Selar and also some money to begin paid marketing.

But I want to give you another option that will help you, so you don't get stuck if much people from your social media audience did not pre-order your product. This strategy involves strategically asking for help.

Here's how it goes…

Create a broadcast list on WhatsApp. I recommend creating about four different broadcast lists: one list for the young men in your contact, another one for the young ladies in your contact, another for the older men or those men you respect in your contact and another for the older ladies or the ladies you respect in your contact.

Each broadcast list can have up to 100 people each. Once it is ready, it's time to send them a message.

You are going to craft a simple message to send to each list, informing them of your new upcoming online course you are about to launch. Let them know that you need their support to cover the cost of completing and launching the project.

Below is a template you can use. You must not use it word for word. It's just a template to help you see how to craft your own message.

Hello ... sir (for the older men), or ma (for the older women), or bro (for the younger men) or dear (for the younger ladies)...

I hope you are doing okay today?

I am chatting you up because I need a favor from you.

I've been working on a project and I am almost done with it. It's an online course that teaches people how to....(insert what your course will teach people).

The reason I contacted you is because I am reaching out to my friends and well-wishers to seek support to cover some compulsory expenses I need to make to complete the project and launch it.

When this course is ready, it will be selling for $15 each (or any amount you hope to sell your course), but I want to ask if you wouldn't mind pre-ordering this course right now to help me raise the money I need to complete the task.

If you decide to help me, you can pay whatever amount you want, starting with $2 and as soon as the project is completed, you will receive an automatic access to this course at no extra cost— guaranteed!

Your support will really mean a lot to me and my vision as it will help speed up the process of getting this job done. Please pay whatever amount you want for the course to pre-order it, starting from $2. See it as a way of supporting me on this project and I'll never take it for granted.

If you have said yes to my request, kindly pay into the account details below.

But if for any reason you are unable to do this for me, please don't feel bad about it. I understand times are not very easy right now and you must have a lot of responsibilities.

(Account details)

Thanks as I anticipate your response!

I have never used this on my contacts personally, but I have helped others raise money to complete their projects using this strategy. If you decide to use it, please do not abuse it and endeavor to fulfill your promise of letting them have the product at no extra cost. This is a test of your integrity, so don't get greedy later.

Now, do the math. Assuming each of the four broadcast lists have 100 people, that means you are sending this message to 400 people.

By giving them an opportunity to get a $15 product at any amount, even as cheap as $2, I am sure that not less than 100 people will take the offer.

Some of them may do it as a favor to you, while others may see it as an opportunity to get your product at a very cheap price.

So, if 100 people pay $2 each to your account; that gives you $200 in cash…more than enough to compete your project and launch it in a big way.

But this will only work if you already have a good relationship with your contacts. People won't answer you if they see you as irresponsible. They might even doubt that it is really you who is sending them the message.

This is why I insist on becoming a person of value. Make sure people know you for the value you provide, especially around your niche. It is even better to create these broadcast lists beforehand and start sharing valuable content with them from time to time.

If people know that you are already an authority in your niche, it will be easy for them to believe you when you announce that you have created a course around your niche. They'll be happy to partake in what you are doing.

Thank you for reading to this point. I hope to see you at the top!

MEET THE AUTHOR

I am one person who has always been in love with the idea of working from home and making money from the comfort of my bedroom.

After losing my first (traditional) business back in 2009, I was broke, hopeless, frustrated and didn't know what else to do with my life. My experience with internet business started the day I saw an ad on a newspaper with the caption, "Income Opportunity With Google". Before then, I never knew there was a way to make money online.

I bundled up the last N10,000 I had and went to the bank to pay for this guide. I didn't even have a laptop or a smartphone, so when the material I paid for was sent to my Email, I had to go to a cyber café to download and print it out. It was a bundle containing 3 eBooks.

I spent the next couple of weeks studying those materials without really understanding what I was expected to do next. Just a bunch of internet jargons I'd never really heard before, like SEO, Adsense, Domain name, Hosting, SSL, etc.

Buying those eBooks didn't make me money, but it opened my eyes to a reality I never had before. I came to realize that it was actually possible to make money from the comfort of my home, leveraging the internet to provide some sort of value that people would be willing to pay for.

So far, I have used the internet to do business and make money in different industries: Network marketing, affiliate marketing, selling of physical products, and even creating and selling digital products.

I started The Kings Organization for the purpose of reaching out to more people who are still trapped in the unemployment—or underemployment—cycle.

My goal is to help people create the lifestyle of their dream by leveraging the same power of financial education and digital marketing skills that gave me my own freedom.

Through The Kings Organization, we will empower thousands of individuals to become masters of money rather than being slaves to it.

www.ingramcontent.com/pod-product-compliance
Lightning Source LLC
Chambersburg PA
CBHW061921270726
48658CB00005BB/1859